Length of table. Estimate: About __2__ metres.

Measure: About __2__ metres.

Use a metre stick. Estimate to the nearest half metre.
Then measure and write your answer in metres and
centimetres:–

1 the width of your
   classroom;

2 the length of your
   classroom;

3 the height of a door;

4 the length of your teacher's
   table;

5 your height;

6 the length of the school hall;

7 the width of the school
   hall;

8 the length of the school
   building.

9 Estimate to the nearest metre:–
   (a) the height of any tree you can see;
   (b) the height of a lamp-post;
   (c) the height of the highest point of your school.

Measuring in yards, feet and inches

Measure each object to the nearest half inch.

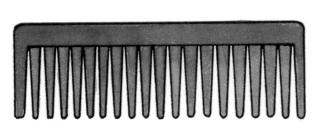

1

_____ inches.

2

_____ inches.

3

_____ inches.

4

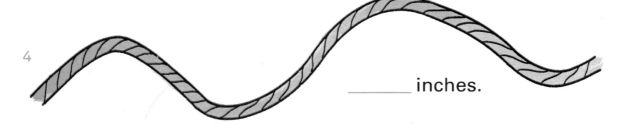

_____ inches.

5

Long side = _____ inches.   Short side = _____ inches.

3 feet = 1 yard

You need a stick or piece of string I yard long.
Mark the three feet on it.

Estimate to the nearest half yard, also to the nearest half foot.
Then measure to the nearest half yard and half foot with your
stick and string.

1 Width of classroom.
   Estimate: _____ yards.   Estimate: _____ feet.
   Measure: _____ yards.   Measure: _____ feet.

2 Length of classroom.
   Estimate: _____ yards.   Estimate: _____ feet.
   Measure: _____ yards.   Measure: _____ feet.

3 Estimate, then measure,
   the length and width of
   the school hall in feet.

	Estimate	Measure
Length		
Width		

Measuring round the edge

How far around each shape?
Measure in centimetres.

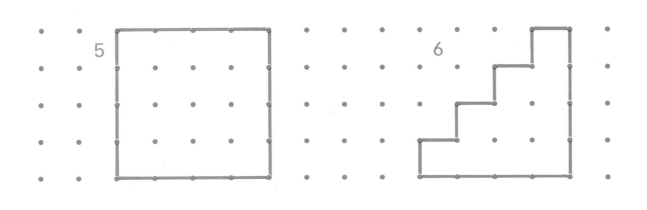

How long is each side?
Find the perimeter of each shape.
Copy and complete each table.

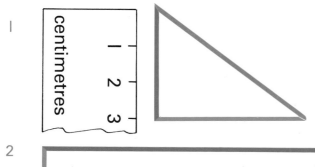

side	centimetres
	3
total	

2

side	centimetres
total	

3

side	centimetres
total	

4

side	centimetres
total	

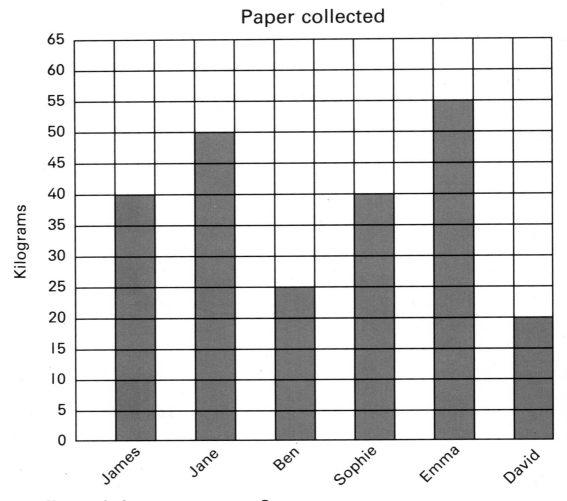

Paper collected

1 Who collected the most paper?

2 Who collected the least paper?

3 How much did Ben collect?

4 Who collected more than Sophie?

5 Who collected as much as Sophie?

6 Who collected 55 kilograms of paper?

7 How much did Ben and Emma collect together?

8 How much more did James collect than David?

How much milk?

1  Milk ½ Pint, Milk ½ Pint, Milk ½ Pint

2 Milk 1 Pint, Milk 1 Pint, Milk 1 Pint

3 Milk ½ Pint, Milk ½ Pint, Milk ½ Pint, Milk ½ Pint, Milk ½ Pint

4 Milk ½ Pint, Milk ½ Pint

5 Milk 1 Pint, Milk 1 Pint

6 Milk 1 Pint, Milk ½ Pint, Milk ½ Pint, Milk 1 Pint

7 Milk 1 Pint, Milk 1 Pint, Milk 1 Pint, Milk 1 Pint

8 Milk 1 Pint, Milk 1 Pint, Milk ½ Pint

9 Milk 1 Pint, Milk ½ Pint, Milk ½ Pint

10 Milk 1 Pint, Milk 1 Pint, Milk ½ Pint, Milk ½ Pint, Milk ½ Pint

11 Milk 1 Pint, Milk 1 Pint, Milk ½ Pint, Milk ½ Pint, Milk ½ Pint, Milk ½ Pint

12 Milk 1 Pint, Milk ½ pint

keeping skills sharp

1 How much?

2 How much?

Tens and units addition

Add.

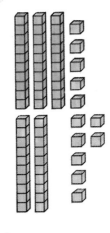

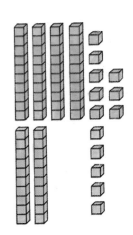

1. 35
    + 27
    62

2. 48
    + 25
    73

3. 29
    + 37
    66

4. 16
    + 64
    80

5. 25
    + 46
    71

6. 38
    + 27
    65

7. 48
    + 32
    80

8. 51
    + 19
    70

9. 23
    + 68
    91

10. 27
    + 14
    41

11. 45
    + 45
    90

12. 57
    + 35
    92

13. 78
    + 19
    97

14. 36
    + 48
    84

15. 57
    + 27
    84

16. 36
    + 45
    81

17. 38
    + 38
    76

18. 27
    + 27
    54

19. 46
    + 46
    92

20. 38
    + 14
    52

21. 38
    + 34
    72

22. 38
    + 44
    82

23. 47
    + 18
    65

24. 47
    + 28
    75

25. 47
    + 38
    85

26. 47
    + 48
    95

27. 29
    + 52
    81

Add.

1. 35
    + 29
    64

2. 44
    + 27

3. 35
    + 36
    71

4. 48
    + 25
    73

5. 46
    + 29
    75

6. 35
    + 35
    70

7. 19
    + 35
    54

8. 19
    + 45
    64

9. 58
    + 23
    81

10. 32
    + 28
    60

11. 66
    + 19
    85

12. 27
    + 54
    81

13. 75
    + 19
    94

14. 24
    + 67
    91

15. 37
    + 21
    58

16. 46
    + 38
    84

17. 52
    + 46
    98

18. 37
    + 44
    81

19. 83
    + 8
    91

20. 61
    + 9
    70

21. 45
    + 7
    52

22. 67
    + 9
    76

1	28 + 34	2	34 + 9	3	57 + 36	4	44 + 36	5	53 + 8

6	53 + 15	7	58 + 34	8	25 + 32	9	17 + 60	10	18 + 53

11	28 + 48	12	21 + 56	13	17 + 38	14	7 + 28	15	32 + 58

$$\begin{array}{r} 53 \\ +\ 9 \\ \hline 62 \end{array}$$

$53 + 10 = 63$
$63 - 1 = 62$

I have a shortcut for adding 9.
First add 10. That's easy.
Then subtract 1. That's easy, too.

Try the shortcut.

16	47 + 9	17	67 + 9	18	84 + 9	19	35 + 9	20	29 + 9

Copy and complete in two ways.

28 + 25 = <u>5 3</u>

$$\begin{array}{r} 2\overset{2}{8} \\ +\ 2\ 5 \\ \hline 5\ 3 \\ \overset{}{\scriptstyle 1} \end{array}$$

1 53 + 19 = ___

2 32 + 57 = ___

3 19 + 53 = ___

4 46 + 32 = ___

5 42 + 49 = ___

6 54 + 38 = ___

7 38 + 38 = ___

8 56 + 36 = ___

9 53 + 26 = ___

Addition puzzles

Copy the grid on squared paper.
Then complete the puzzle.

A 5	B 2			C 9	
D			E	3	
		F			
G	H			I	
J					

Across	Down
A 40 + 12	A 50 + 8
D 59 + 28	B 14 + 13
E 21 + 22	C 51 + 42
F 48 + 48	E 40 + 6
G 50 + 25	G 35 + 37
I 10 + 6	H 25 + 25
J 8 + 12	I 3 + 10

62	93	42	78	35	81	53	27	73	61
A	F	I	K	L	O	R	S	T	W

Why do ducks fly south in winter?
Copy and complete to find the answer.

28 + 14	65 + 8
42	
I	

35 + 7	18 + 9

43 + 30	64 + 17	58 + 23

46 + 47	28 + 34	37 + 16

48 + 25	38 + 43

26 + 35	41 + 21	17 + 18	59 + 19

Addition problems

Find the totals.

Bottles collected			
Name	First Week	Second Week	Total
Bob	20	30	
Susie	32	14	
Emma	43	29	
Becky	33	25	
Pavlos	46	28	
Ben	42	39	

Bottles collected			
Name	First Week	Second Week	Total
Sarah	35	26	
Mark	47	38	
Ann	44	34	
William	27	45	
Tom	37	41	
Olga	24	36	

keeping skills sharp

Find the number that is 1 more.

1 38,____   2 49,____   3 65,____   4 74,____

5 42,____   6 37,____   7 70,____   8 89,____

Copy onto squared paper. Fill in the missing numbers.

Add across.
Add down.

Example:

	+		=
+	20	8	28
	20	1	21
=	40	9	49

1

	+		=
+	10	6	
	60	8	
=			

2

	+		=
+	30	5	
	50	9	
=			

3

	+		=
+	30	7	
	10	6	
=			

4

	+		=
+	20	3	
	40	9	
=			

5

	+		=
+	30	7	
	40	6	
=			

6

	+		=
+	50	5	
	40	2	
=			

7

	+		=
+	40	8	
	40	8	
=			

8

	+		=
+	20	7	
	60	5	
=			

9

	+		=
+	30	7	
	50	8	
=			

Adding money

Give the total cost.

1 	2 	3 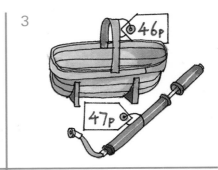
46p 38p	47p 29p	46p 47p
4 	5 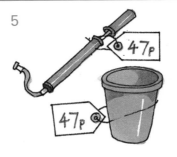	6 
29p 38p	47p 47p	46p 29p
7 	8 	9 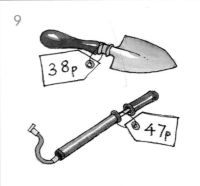
29p 29p	46p 47p	38p 47p

Find the total cost.
Write the sum.
Draw the coins you need.

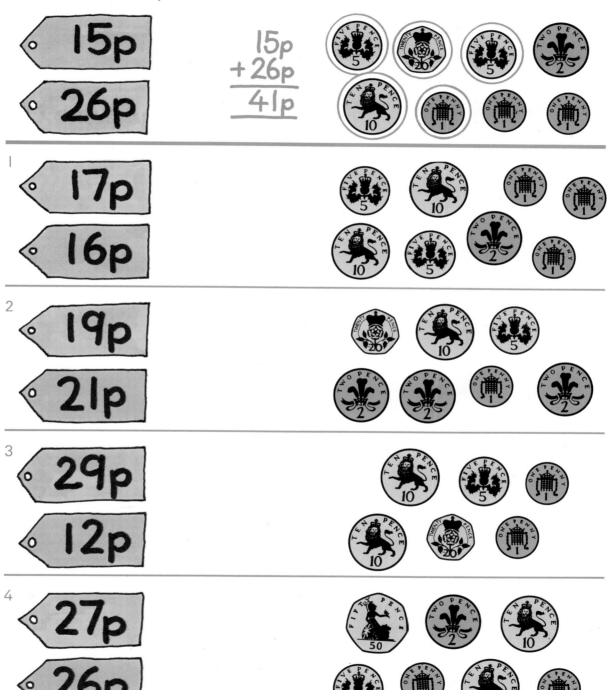

15p
+ 26p
41p

1   17p   16p

2   19p   21p

3   29p   12p

4   27p   26p

Tens and units subtraction

Need more units.

$$\begin{array}{r} 63 \\ -26 \\ \hline 37 \end{array}$$

Regroup I ten for 10 units.

$$\begin{array}{r} {}^5\!\cancel{6}3 \\ -26 \\ \hline 37 \end{array}$$

Subtract!

$$\begin{array}{r} {}^5\!\cancel{6}3 \\ -26 \\ \hline 37 \end{array}$$

Subtract.

1 61 − 28 3̶83	2 32 − 19 13	3 43 − 27 16	4 75 − 18 57	5 90 − 36 54	6 74 − 35 39
7 65 − 48 17	8 62 − 19 43	9 46 − 38 08	10 81 − 26 55	11 71 − 53 18	12 52 − 19 33
13 60 − 46 14	14 63 − 59 04	15 72 − 26 46	16 64 − 27 37	17 85 − 36 49	18 93 − 44 49

keeping skills sharp

Write the time.

1

2

3

Do not need more units, so subtract.

```
  58
  23
  35
```

Do need more units, so regroup and subtract.

```
  6
  7̶1
- 46
  25
```

1.
```
  48
- 15
  33
```

2.
```
  53
- 27
  36
```

3.
```
  64
- 56
   8
```

4.
```
  90
- 38
  52
```

5.
```
  81
- 35
  46
```

6.
```
  58
- 19
  39
```

7.
```
  66
- 58
   8
```

8.
```
  63
- 27
  36
```

9.
```
  37
- 18
  19
```

10.
```
  53
- 39
  14
```

11.
```
  40
- 22
```

12.
```
  40
- 32
```

13.
```
  83
- 47
```

14.
```
  62
- 11
```

15.
```
  38
-  6
```

16.
```
  92
- 48
```

17.
```
  43
- 39
```

18.
```
  64
- 55
```

19.
```
  74
- 34
```

20.
```
  33
-  5
```

21.
```
  50
- 24
```

22.
```
  66
- 38
```

23.
```
  76
- 58
```

24.
```
  42
- 18
```

25.
```
  79
- 25
```

26.
```
  75
- 57
```

27.
```
  47
- 29
```

28.
```
  80
- 47
```

29.
```
  38
-  9
```

30.
```
  73
- 49
```

Money problems

Find the total cost of:

 and I

$$
\begin{array}{r}
35p \\
+\ 20p \\
\hline
55p \\
\end{array}
$$

---

1 I and I

2 I and I

3 I and I

4 I and I

5 I  and I

6 I  and I

7 2

8 2

9 2

10 2

11 2

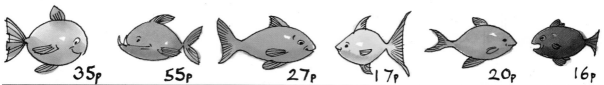

had	bought	had left
		$\begin{array}{r} 3\,4\,1\,p \\ -\ 2\,7\,p \\ \hline 1\,4\,p \end{array}$

How much money left?

	had	bought
1		
2		
3		
4		
5		

0	5	10								

 35p

 43p

$$\frac{\overset{3}{\cancel{4}}3_p - 35_p}{8_p}$$

How much more does cost?

 28p

 49p

What is the total cost?

2

 53p

 42p

How much more for  ?

3

58p

36p

What is the total cost?

4

 56p

 18p

How much less for ？

5

47p

35p

How much more for ？

Multiplication

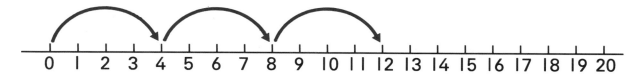

 (a) 4 + 4 + 4 = 12

(b)　　3 fours = 12

(c)　　4 × 3 = 12

How many?

1

(a) 2 + 2 + 2 + 2 + 2 = ___

(b)　　　　5 twos = ___

(c)　　　　2 × 5 = ___

2

(a)　　　　5 + 5 = ___

(b)　　　　2 fives = ___

(c)　　　　5 × 2 = ___

3

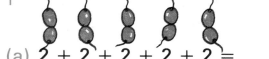

(a)　　2 + 2 + 2 + 2 = ___

(b)　　　　4 twos = ___

(c)　　　　2 × 4 = ___

4

(a)　　　　4 + 4 = ___

(b)　　　　2 fours = ___

(c)　　　　4 × 2 = ___

5

(a) 3 + 3 + 3 + 3 + 3 = ___

(b)　　　　5 threes = ___

(c)　　　　3 × 5 = ___

6

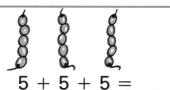

(a)　　　5 + 5 + 5 = ___

(b)　　　　3 fives = ___

(c)　　　　5 × 3 = ___

0 1 2 3 4 5 6 7 8 9 10 11 12 13 14 15 16 17 18 19 20

Copy and complete.

$$\begin{array}{r} 2 \\ \times 1 \\ \hline 2 \end{array}$$

2 multiplied by 1 is 2

$$\begin{array}{r} 1 \\ \times 2 \\ \hline 2 \end{array}$$

1 multiplied by 2 is 2

1

$$\begin{array}{r} 2 \\ \times 2 \\ \hline \end{array}$$

2 multiplied by ___ is ___

2

$$\begin{array}{r} 2 \\ \times 3 \\ \hline \end{array}$$

2 multiplied by ___ is ___

3

$$\begin{array}{r} 3 \\ \times 2 \\ \hline \end{array}$$

___ multiplied by ___ is ___

4

$$\begin{array}{r} 2 \\ \times 4 \\ \hline \end{array}$$

___ multiplied by ___ is ___

5

$$\begin{array}{r} 4 \\ \times 2 \\ \hline \end{array}$$

___ multiplied by ___ is ___

6

$$\begin{array}{r} 2 \\ \times 5 \\ \hline \end{array}$$

___ multiplied by ___ is ___

7

$$\begin{array}{r} 5 \\ \times 2 \\ \hline \end{array}$$

___ multiplied by ___ is ___

| 0 | 1 | 2 | 3 | 4 | 5 | 6 | 7 | 8 | 9 | 10 | 11 | 12 | 13 | 14 | 15 | 16 | 17 | 18 | 19 | 20 |

Multiply.

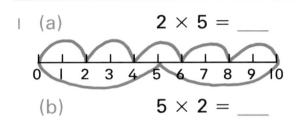

$\begin{array}{r} 2 \\ \times 3 \\ \hline 6 \end{array}$ Two in each set.
Three sets.
Six altogether.

$2 \times 3 = 6$

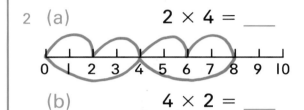

$\begin{array}{r} 3 \\ \times 2 \\ \hline 6 \end{array}$ Three in each set.
Two sets.
Six altogether.

$3 \times 2 = 6$

Copy and complete:

1 (a) $2 \times 5 =$ ___

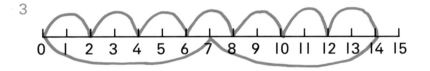

0 1 2 3 4 5 6 7 8 9 10

(b) $5 \times 2 =$ ___

2 (a) $2 \times 4 =$ ___

0 1 2 3 4 5 6 7 8 9 10

(b) $4 \times 2 =$ ___

3

0 1 2 3 4 5 6 7 8 9 10 11 12 13 14 15

(a) $2 \times 7 =$ ___

(b) $7 \times 2 =$ ___

4 **Find the jumps on the line. Find the missing numbers.**

0 1 2 3 4 5 6 7 8 9 10 11 12 13 14 15

(a) $2 \times 6 =$ ___

(b) $6 \times 2 =$ ___

5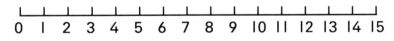

(a) $\begin{array}{r} 2 \\ \times 8 \\ \hline \end{array}$

(b) $2 \times 8 =$ ___

6

(a) $\begin{array}{r} 10 \\ \times 2 \\ \hline \end{array}$

(b) $10 \times 2 =$ ___

Three as a factor

Copy and complete:

1

$1 \times 3 =$ ___ $\begin{array}{r} 1 \\ \times 3 \\ \hline \end{array}$ $3 \times 1 =$ ___ $\begin{array}{r} 3 \\ \times 1 \\ \hline \end{array}$

1 multiplied by 3 = ___   3 multiplied by 1 = ___

$1 \times 3 =$ ___ $3 \times 1 =$ ___

2

$3 \times 5 =$ ___ $\begin{array}{r} 3 \\ \times 5 \\ \hline \end{array}$ 3 multiplied by 5 = ___

$3 \times 5 =$ ___

$5 \times 3 =$ ___ $\begin{array}{r} 5 \\ \times 3 \\ \hline \end{array}$ 5 multiplied by 3 = ___

$5 \times 3 =$ ___

3 Each has 3 sides.

How many sides for
(a) 2 triangles ___   (b) 3 triangles ___
(c) 4 triangles ___   (d) 5 triangles ___

Four as a factor

Copy and complete:

1

1 × 4 = ___   1
              × 4
              ____

4 × 1 = ___   4
              × 1
              ____

1 multiplied by 4 = ___   4 multiplied by 1 = ___

2

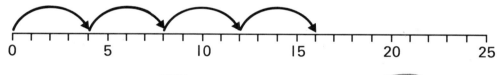

4 × 4 = ___   4
              × 4
              ____

4 multiplied by 4 = ___

3 Each has 4 sides.

How many sides for
(a) 2 squares ___   (b) 3 squares ___
(c) 4 squares ___   (d) 5 squares ___

Five as a factor

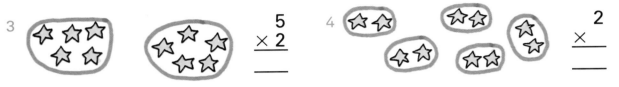

Copy and complete:

1 ⭐⭐⭐⭐⭐ $\times \dfrac{5}{1}$

___ multiplied by ___ is___

2 ⭐⭐⭐⭐⭐ $\times \dfrac{1}{5}$

___ multiplied by ___ is___

3 ⭐⭐⭐ ⭐⭐⭐⭐ $\times \dfrac{5}{2}$

___ multiplied by ___ is___

4 ⭐⭐ ⭐⭐ ⭐⭐ ⭐⭐ ⭐⭐ $\times \dfrac{2}{}$

___ multiplied by ___ is___

5 ⭐⭐⭐⭐⭐ ⭐⭐⭐⭐⭐ ⭐⭐⭐⭐⭐ $\times \dfrac{5}{3}$

___ multiplied by ___ is___

6 ⭐⭐⭐ ⭐⭐⭐ ⭐⭐⭐ ⭐⭐⭐ ⭐⭐⭐ $\times$ ___

___ multiplied by ___ is___

7 ⭐⭐⭐⭐⭐ ⭐⭐⭐⭐⭐ ⭐⭐⭐⭐⭐ ⭐⭐⭐⭐⭐ $\times$ ___

___ multiplied by ___ is___

8 ⭐⭐⭐⭐ ⭐⭐⭐⭐ ⭐⭐⭐⭐ ⭐⭐⭐⭐ ⭐⭐⭐⭐ $\times$ ___

___ multiplied by ___ is___

9 ⭐⭐⭐⭐⭐ ⭐⭐⭐⭐⭐ ⭐⭐⭐⭐⭐ ⭐⭐⭐⭐⭐ ⭐⭐⭐⭐⭐ $\times$ ___

___ multiplied by ___ is___

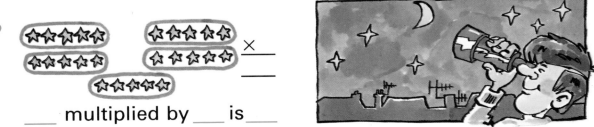

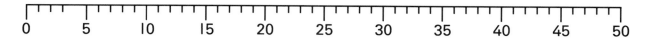

 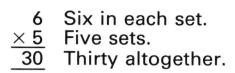

6 Six in each set.
× 5 Five sets.
30 Thirty altogether.

$6 \times 5 = 30$

5 Five in each set.
× 6 Six sets.
30 Thirty altogether.

$5 \times 6 = 30$

1 How many? Write the sum.   2 How many? Write the sum.

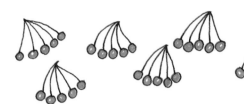

×
___

×
___

Draw cherries to show these sums.
Write the sums by the cherries.

3   5   4   2   5   5   6   3
     × 2   × 5   × 8   × 5
     ___   ___   ___   ___

7   5   8   4   9   10   10   5
     × 9   × 5   × 5   × 5
     ___   ___   ___   ___

11 $5 \times 10 = $ ___   12 $1 \times 5 = $ ___

Multiplication problems

Find:

1

the cost of 5

2

the cost of 7

3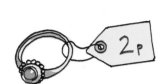

the cost of 8

4

the cost of 4

5

the cost of 4

6

the cost of 2

7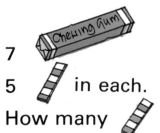

7
5 in each.
How many ?

8

2
9 in each.
How many ?

9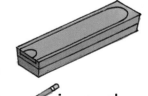

4
8 in each.
How many ?

10

4
10 in each.
How many ?

Find the cost.

1 4 🐑

2 8 🧸

3 9 🐘

4 7 🐑

5 6 🧸

6 9 🐷

7 8 🐑

8 10 🐘

9 5 🐷

10 How much do 4 🐑 and 2 🧸 cost?

11 How much do 8 🐘 and 5 🐷 cost?

12 Luke had 50p.
He bought 9 🐘 .
How much money did he have left?

13 Lisa had 80p.
She bought 6 🐷 .
How much money did she have left?

14 Bill had 40p.
He bought 10 🐑 .
How much money did he have left?

15 Tom had 90p.
He bought 8 🧸 .
How much money did he have left?

Changing the order of multiplication

You can change the order
and the answer stays the same.

$5 \times 2 = 10$ $2 \times 5 = 10$

$4 \times 3 = 12$ $3 \times 4 = 12$

Multiply.

1 (a) $4 \times 1 =$ ___   2 (a) $2 \times 1 =$ ___   3 (a) $5 \times 1 =$ ___

  (b) $1 \times 4 =$ ___   (b) $1 \times 2 =$ ___   (b) $1 \times 5 =$ ___

4 (a) $8 \times 1 =$ ___   5 (a) $3 \times 1 =$ ___   6 (a) $6 \times 2 =$ ___

  (b) $1 \times 8 =$ ___   (b) $1 \times 3 =$ ___   (b) $2 \times 6 =$ ___

7 (a) $2 \times 4 =$ ___   8 (a) $3 \times 2 =$ ___   9 (a) $9 \times 1 =$ ___

  (b) $4 \times 2 =$ ___   (b) $2 \times 3 =$ ___   (b) $1 \times 9 =$ ___

keeping skills sharp

Estimate then measure these lengths.

1    2

Multiply.

1 3 × 5	2 8 × 5	3 5 × 4	4 4 × 4	5 5 × 6	6 1 × 5
7 4 × 6	8 7 × 3	9 4 × 3	10 3 × 4	11 3 × 9	12 7 × 4
13 3 × 6	14 5 × 3	15 4 × 8	16 2 × 5	17 5 × 7	18 3 × 3

How many squares?

19   20    21

22   23   24

25    26    27

Who am I?

28   If you multiply me by 4, you get 12.

29   If you multiply me by 9 you get 27.

30   If you multiply a number by me you get the same number.

31   If you multiply me by 2 and then add 1 to the product you get 9.

More multiplication

My score
is 6.

Find each score.

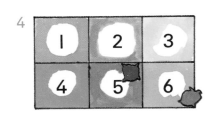

15

Find each score as you did on page 34.

1
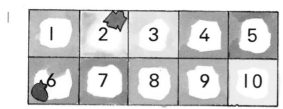

2

3

4

Copy and complete this multiplication table.

5

X	1	2	3	4	5	6	7	8	9	10
1								8		
2					10					
3										
4										
5									45	

Multiplying money

Find the total cost.

5 the cost is 10p

2

3

4

1

6

7

8

6

10

9

1

8

3

10

5

2

7

3

9

4

11

5

Telling the time

Write the times.

6:05

Give the time.

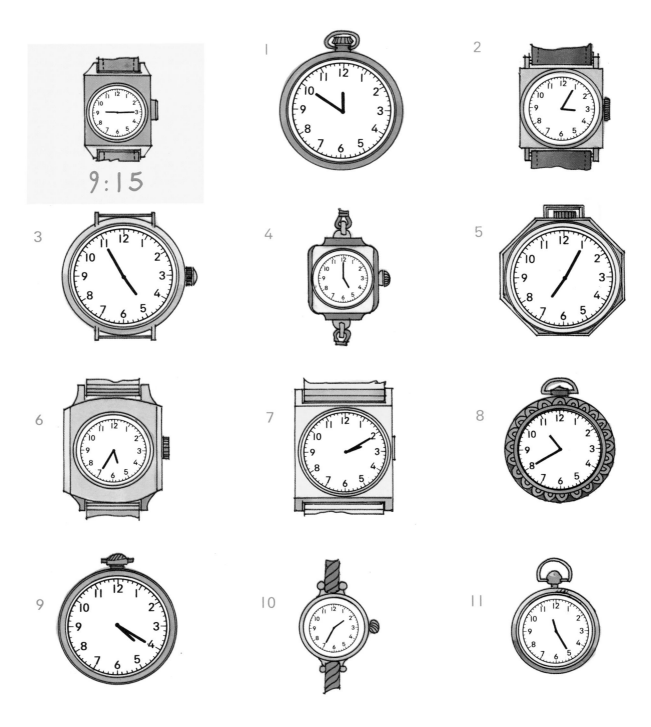

9:15

Backwards and forwards in time

Find each time.

(a) I hour ago **now** (b) 2 hours from now

3:00 **6:00**

I

(a) 2 hours ago **now** (b) 2 hours from now

2

(a) 3 hours ago **now** (b) 4 hours from now

3

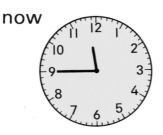

(a) 4 hours ago **now** (b) 2 hours from now

4

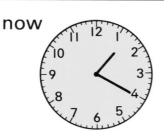

(a) 3 hours ago **now** (b) 5 hours from now

Hundreds, tens and units

How many? Copy and complete.

	hundreds	tens	units	
	5	6	7	567

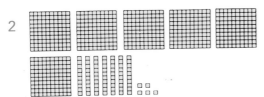

	hundreds	tens	units
1			

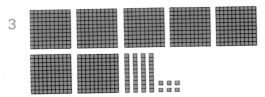

	hundreds	tens	units
2			

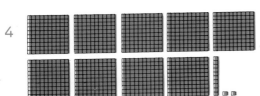

	hundreds	tens	units
3			

	hundreds	tens	units
4			

keeping skills sharp

1	2	3	4	5	6
3	6	3	8	3	2
5	3	5	1	4	7
+ 8	+ 2	+ 5	+ 9	+ 9	+ 8
___	___	___	___	___	___

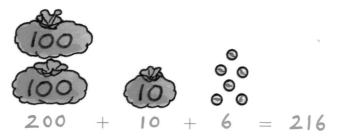

$$200 + 10 + 6 = 216$$

How many marbles?
Write your answers as shown above.

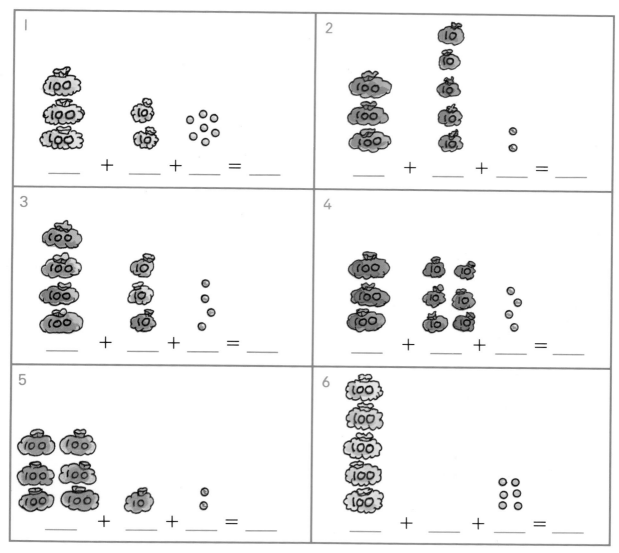

1

___ + ___ + ___ = ___

2

___ + ___ + ___ = ___

3

___ + ___ + ___ = ___

4

___ + ___ + ___ = ___

5

___ + ___ + ___ = ___

6

___ + ___ + ___ = ___

Ordering numbers

Write the numbers in order.

| 163 | 164 | 165 | 166 | 167 | 168 |

Copy and complete.

1 | 258 | | 260 | | | |

2 | 426 | | | | | 431 |

3 | 507 | | | | | 512 |

4 | | 598 | | | 601 | |

5 | 697 | | | | 701 | |

6 | | 799 | | | | 803 |

7 | | 900 | | 902 | | |

8 | | | 997 | | | 1000 |

10 less

10 more

124

144

What number is 10 more?

136:   146 is 10 more than 136

1 (a) 115   (b) 138   (c) 156   (d) 206

2 (a) 220   (b) 369   (c) 400   (d) 35

3 (a) 83   (b) 567   (c) 790   (d) 100

4 (a) 891   (b) 237   (c) 301   (d) 99

What number is 10 less?

123:   113 is 10 less than 123

1 (a) 142   (b) 258   (c) 30   (d) 11

2 (a) 302   (b) 46   (c) 500   (d) 196

3 (a) 517   (b) 601   (c) 909   (d) 22

4 (a) 700   (b) 222   (c) 301   (d) 73

What number is 100 more?

316: 416 is 100 more than 316

1	(a) 385	(b) 213	(c) 452	(d) 271
2	(a) 163	(b) 674	(c) 85	(d) 196
3	(a) 867	(b) 142	(c) 92	(d) 731
4	(a) 9	(b) 899	(c) 19	(d) 48

What number is 100 less?

532: 432 is 100 less than 532

1	(a) 182	(b) 356	(c) 250	(d) 342
2	(a) 135	(b) 536	(c) 700	(d) 299
3	(a) 153	(b) 609	(c) 863	(d) 450
4	(a) 106	(b) 201	(c) 337	(d) 936

keeping skills sharp

1	2	3	4	5	6
5	3	1	4	2	3
× 2	× 6	× 9	× 7	× 8	× 5

Adding and subtracting tens

In what way
is a baby like
a good
footballer?

Find the answer to each question below, then write down the
letter for each one. They will give you the answer to the riddle.
* shows the end of a word.

A	B	C	D	E	F	G	H	I	J	K	L	M
	90		10	30			80	60			100	
N	O	P	Q	R	S	T	U	V	W	X	Y	Z
	70			50		40					20	

The answer to question I is 40. T is the letter for 40.
So T is the first letter.

1 10 less than 50

2 20 less than 100

3 50 less than 80

4 40 less than 60*

5 70 more than 20

6 40 more than 30

7 20 more than 20

8 50 more than 30*

9 90 minus 80

10 80 minus 30

11 70 minus 10

12 60 plus 30

13 10 plus 80

14 50 plus 50

15 10 + 10 + 10*

> and <

148 comes
before 152.

161 comes
after 158.

146 147 148 149 150 151 152 153 154 155 156 157 158 159 160 161 162 163

148 < 152
is less than

161 > 158
is greater than

Copy and complete using < or >.

1 132 ◯ 150
is less than

2 256 ◯ 250
is greater than

3 99 ◯ 100
is less than

4 99 ◯ 103
is less than

5 206 ◯ 305
is less than

6 390 ◯ 389
is greater than

7 248 ◯ 348
is less than

8 246 ◯ 264
is less than

9 502 ◯ 486
is greater than

10 600 ◯ 593

11 476 ◯ 467

12 449 ◯ 450

13 800 ◯ 799

14 300 ◯ 201

15 684 ◯ 679

16 792 ◯ 776

17 457 ◯ 556

18 657 ◯ 675

19 901 ◯ 897

20 697 ◯ 702

21 988 ◯ 899

1   James scored 139.
Gemma scores 140.
Who scored more?

Write two number sentences with each pair of numbers.
Use < and >.

2	148	137 < 148	3	153	4	155	5	152	6	162
	137	148 > 137		146		151		163		185

7	173	8	117	9	185	10	190	11	190	12	187
	151		120		160		189		191		165

Answer.

Rover   Duke

13 Nick is 28 years old.
Jill is 52 years old.
Who is older?

14 Ben is 153 centimetres tall.
Tom is 163 centimetres tall.
Who is taller?

15 Rover is 45 centimetres tall.
Duke is 53 centimetres tall.
Which is shorter?

16 Lucy scored 116 points.
Vicky scored 114 points.
Who scored more?

17 Mandy read 123 pages.
Wayne read 142 pages.
Who read more?

These are called digits.

| 0 | 1 | 2 | 3 | 4 | 5 | 6 | 7 | 8 | 9 |

Here are two digits: 3 8

They can be used to build
these two-digit numbers: 38 83

1 List the three-digit numbers
you can build with these
digits:

2 What was the greatest number you built?

3 What was the least number you built?

4 List the three-digit numbers you
can build with these digits: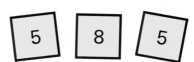

5 What was the greatest number?

6 What was the least number?

Fractions of numbers

$\frac{1}{2}$ is coloured.

$\frac{1}{2}$ is called 'half'.

$\frac{1}{4}$ is coloured.

$\frac{1}{4}$ is called 'quarter'.

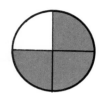

$\frac{3}{4}$ is coloured.

$\frac{3}{4}$ is called 'three quarters'.

---

1 What fraction is coloured?
Give your answer as: $\frac{1}{2}$, $\frac{1}{4}$, $\frac{3}{4}$ or 'some other fraction'

(a)

(b)

(c)

(d)

(e)

(f)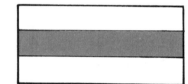

2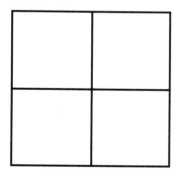

Trace or draw this square.

(a) Colour half of it red.
Colour a quarter of it blue.

(b) What fraction is not coloured?

3 $\frac{1}{4}$ of the garden is lawn.
What fraction is not lawn?

1 of the 4 sweets is round.

$\frac{1}{4}$ of the sweets is round.

3 of the 4 sweets are square.

$\frac{3}{4}$ of the sweets are square.

2 of the 4 sweets are toffees.

$\frac{1}{2}$ of the sweets is toffees.

2 of the 4 sweets are not toffees.

$\frac{1}{2}$ of the sweets is not toffees.

For each set write the fraction   (a)   in the loop

                                            (b)   not in the loop.

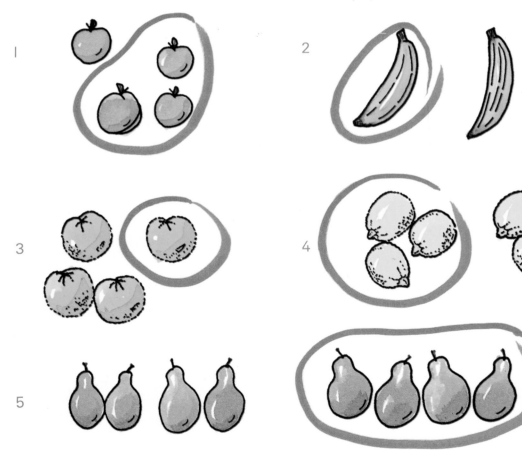

1

2

3

4

5

Addition and subtraction are related.

4, 6 and 10 are a family of facts.

6 + 4 = 10
4 + 6 = 10
10 − 4 = 6
10 − 6 = 4

Give each family of facts.

1

2

3

4

Use numbers in two addition equations and
two subtraction equations.

5

6

7

8

9

10

Subtraction facts

Subtraction by
taking away.

$12 - 3 = 9$

Subtraction by
adding on.

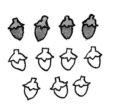

$4 + \underline{} = 11$

$11 - 4 = 7$

I have 4 nuts. How many
more to make 11?

Subtract.

1 $12 - 5 = \underline{}$

2 $11 - 5 = \underline{}$

3 $13 - 4 = \underline{}$

4 $12 - 7 = \underline{}$

$7 + \underline{} = 12$

5 $13 - 8 = \underline{}$

$8 + \underline{} = 13$

6 $11 - 9 = \underline{}$

$9 + \underline{} = 11$

---

7 $12 - 8 =$

10 $17 - 8 =$

13 $14 - 8 =$

16 $14 - 9 =$

19 $11 - 6 =$

8 $13 - 6 = \underline{}$

11 $16 - 8 = \underline{}$

14 $11 - 8 = \underline{}$

17 $16 - 7 = \underline{}$

20 $15 - 7 = \underline{}$

9 $12 - 6 = \underline{}$

12 $15 - 9 = \underline{}$

15 $17 - 9 = \underline{}$

18 $15 - 8 = \underline{}$

21 $11 - 7 = \underline{}$

Subtraction problems

1 Jan made 50

She ate 14

How many

did she have left?

2 Daren made 44

He ate 9

How many

did he have left?

3 Susan made 61

She gave away 18

How many

did she have left?

4 Barry made 76

He sold 28

How many

did he have left?

5 Shelley made 82

She burnt 16

How many

did she have left?

6 David made 90

He gave 22

to his dog.

How many

did he have left?

Ordinal numbers

Write the position of each bird.

The  is _eighth, 8th._

1 The 🐦 is _____. 2 The 🐦 is _____. 3 The 🐦 is _____.

4 The 🐦 is _____. 5 The 🐦 is _____. 6 The 🐦 is _____.

7 Which floor is 2 floors above the sixth floor?

8 Which floor is 2 floors below the ninth floor?

9 The tenth floor is how many floors above the fifth floor?

10 Start on the ground floor, go up 5 floors and then down 3 floors. Where do you end?

Odd and even numbers

Revision   **Even numbers** can be put in 2s.

 12 is even.

Odd numbers have 1 left over when put in 2s.

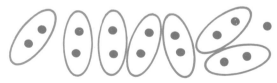 15 is odd.

1	2	3	4	5	6	7	8	9	10
odd	even	odd	even	odd	even	odd	even	odd	even

11	12	13	14	15	16	17	18	19	20
odd	even	odd	even	odd	even	odd	even	odd	even

1   Add 1 to an odd number you always get an even number. Why?
Add 1 to an even number you always get an odd number. Why?
Discuss your answers with your teacher.

2   3 + 6 = 9   8 + 9 = 17
   odd + even = odd   even + odd = odd

Add these. Are the answers odd or even?
(a) 11 + 6   (b) 19 + 8   (c) 14 + 3   (d) 7 + 12
(e) Try adding other numbers where one is odd and the
     other is even. You will find the answers are always odd
     numbers. Why? Discuss your answer with your teacher.

3   Find whether the answers are odd or even when
   (a) you add two even numbers.
   (b) you add two odd numbers.

1

3 is **odd**.   3 + 3 = 6.   6 is **even**.
3 + 3 + 3 = 9.   9 is **odd**.
3 + 3 + 3 + 3 = 12.   12 is **even**.
3 + 3 + 3 + 3 + 3 = 15.   15 is **odd**.

3	6	9	12	15	18	21	24
odd	even	odd	even	odd	even	odd	even

Can you see why, each time you add 3, the number changes
from odd to even or from even to odd?
Discuss your answer with your teacher.

2

5	10	15	20	25
odd	even	odd	even	odd

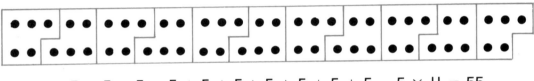

5 + 5 + 5 + 5 + 5 + 5 + 5 + 5 + 5 + 5 + 5 = 5 × 11 = 55
55 is odd.

5	10	15	20	25	30	35	40	45	50	55
odd	even	odd	even	odd	even	odd	even	odd	even	odd

Can you see why, each time you add 5, the number
changes from odd to even or from even to odd?
Discuss your answer with your teacher.

3   2, 4, 6, 8, 10, 12, 14.
Continue adding 2s up to 30.
What is the pattern of odd or even numbers?

4   4, 8, 12, 16, 20, 24.
Continue adding 4s up to 52.
What is the pattern of odd or even numbers?

Function machine

1

Function add 10	
Input	output
6	
10	
2	
14	
0	

2

Function add 9	
Input	output
13	
23	
	11
	16
	20

3

Function add 18	
Input	output
17	
34	
	21
	40
	56

4

Function subtract 5	
Input	output
11	
14	
20	
32	
	12

5

Function subtract 20	
Input	output
80	
91	
43	
	3
	15

6

Function subtract 33	
Input	output
88	
50	
42	
	10
	7

Classification

I

Likes apples .	Does not like apples.	
Tina Ranjit	Ben Greg Ann	Likes cherries.
Jerry Ossie Steve	Karen Jackie	Does not like cherries.

Which children: (a) like apples?

(b) like cherries?

(c) do not like apples?

(d) do not like cherries?

(e) like both cherries and apples?

(f) do not like either fruit?

(g) like apples, but do not like cherries?

(h) like cherries, but do not like apples?

2

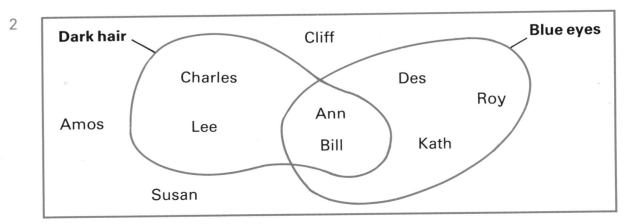

(a) Who has dark hair?

(b) Who has blue eyes?

(c) Who does *not* have blue eyes?

(d) Who has dark hair and blue eyes?

(e) Who does not have blue eyes and does not have fair hair?

Probability

Choose one of these for each answer:

Very likely, likely, unlikely, very unlikely.

Example:

Answer: Very unlikely.

I will live to be 110 years old.

1  I will catch a cold in the next year.	2  I will go for a swim in the next two weeks.
3  I will be married before I am 20 years old.	4  When I am 14 years old I will learn to drive a car.
5  I will have a bath today.	6  Next Christmas I will have a new bicycle.

Cost per person for a week

	May	June	July	August	September
week 1	£150	£155	£160	£170	£155
week 2	£151	£155	£162	£165	£152
week 3	£153	£158	£164	£163	£150
week 4	£154	£158	£165	£160	£148

1 What is the cost of 1 week's holiday
   (a) in week 2, June, (b) in week 4 September,
   (c) in week 1, July?

2 When is (a) the dearest week (the one that costs most)?
            (b) the cheapest week (the one that costs least)?

3 In which weeks are the costs
   (a) £155   (b) £158   (c) £160?

4 Use a calculator to find the cost of the four weeks in
   (a) May   (b) June   (c) July   (d) August   (e) September
   (f) Which of the months is (i) dearest (ii) cheapest?

Competition tables

Round 1	Round 2	Round 3	Round 4
Ed Colin	Ed		
Madge Sal	Sal	Sal	
Mick Tony	Mick		Sal
Donna Sue	Sue	Mick	
Brian Cathy	Brian		Steven
Steven Ann	Steven	Steven	
Maggie Greg	Maggie		Steven
Lee Dot	Lee	Maggie	

1.
(a) How many players entered the competition?
(b) How many players were in Round 2, Round 3, Round 4?
(c) Who played in the final?

2. If there had been 17 players, two would have to play a 'preliminary round'. This would bring the number of players left to 16. What would you do if there were (a) 18 players (b) 19 players?

3. Draw a table for 4 players.
What would you do if there were (a) 5 players (b) 6 players?

1 (a) 20 − 17

  (b) 8 + ☐ = 13

2 Saw 14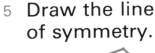
9 flew away.
How many  left?

3
```
   4
   6
 + 7
 ___
```

4 Draw (a) a rectangle
       (b) a square
       (c) a circle
       (d) a triangle.

5 Draw the line
  of symmetry.

6 Measure (a) to the nearest centimetre
  (b) to the nearest inch.

7

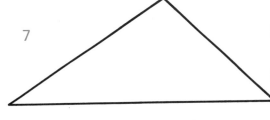

(a) Measure each side of the triangle
    in centimetres.
(b) Find the perimeter of the triangle.

8
```
   48
 + 36
 ____
```

9 (a) 25 + 59
  (b) 64 + 17

10
```
   76
 + 38
 ____
```

11 (a) 40 − 11
   (b) 72 − 43

12 (a) 3 × 5
   (b) 4 × 4

13 (a) 5 fives
   (b) 2 tens

14 (a) 2 multiplied by 10
   (b) 3 multiplied by 4

15 4

10 in each

How many ✏ ?

16

How much for

2 ?

17  (a) How much for 6
(b) Liz had 50p. She bought 3
How much did she have left?

18 How many squares?

19 Copy and complete.

X	2	3	5	10
2				
3				
4				

20 Write the times.

(a) (b)

21 Write the time
(a) I hour before
(b) 2 hours later.

22 How many?

23 Write the next numbers 398 [ ] [ ] [ ] 402 [ ]

24 What number is (a) 10 more than 167
(b) 10 less than 108

25 What number is (a) 100 more than 432
(b) 100 less than 432

26 Copy and complete using > or <.
(a) 98 ◯ 103   (b) 460 ◯ 399   (c) 711 ◯ 688

27 Vicky had 163 stamps. Ali had 159 stamps.
Who had the most stamps?

28 (a) List the six 3 digit numbers you can make.

using $\boxed{2}$, $\boxed{6}$ and $\boxed{5}$.

(b) What was the greatest number you made?
(c) What was the smallest number you made?

29 Draw this: (a) Colour half of the circle red.
(b) Colour a quarter of the circle blue.

30  Find (a) $\frac{1}{2}$ of 8

(b) $\frac{1}{4}$ of 8

(c) $\frac{3}{4}$ of 8.

31 Make two addition equations and two subtraction equations
using 15, 19 and 34.

32 Dave had 80 comics. He gave 37 of them away.
How many did he have left?

33 There are 12 floors in a hotel.
Which floor is (a) 3 floors above the 8th floor
(a) 4 floors above the 6th floor?

34 (a) Is 23 − 16 odd or even?   (b) is 29 + 15 odd or even?

35

	Brown hair	Black hair
Green eyes	Bill Ann	Charles Carol
Brown eyes	Andy	Di Steve

Who has (a) black hair and brown eyes
(b) green eyes and black hair?

36 **Answer very likely, likely, unlikely or very unlikely.**
When I am 50 years old I will have a grandchild.

37 Make up a knockout competition table for 8 players.